Riddles

The big book of riddles for clever kids

Table of Contents

Introduction 1

Riddles 2

Answers 28

Conclusion 51

Introduction

Thank you for choosing this book of riddles!

This book contains over 100 carefully picked, fun, and challenging riddles for kids of all ages. These riddles are perfect for the whole family and will keep you entertained for hours!

This book is split into two sections:

- The first section contains all of the riddles.

- The second section contains all of the answers.

All of the riddles are all numbered, so you can easily flip between the riddles and their answers!

Once again, thanks for picking up this book, I hope you enjoy it!

Riddles

1. What's the two things you can never eat for Breakfast?

2. Why do bees hum?

3. You will buy me to eat, but never eat me. What am I?

4. What can you serve, but never eat?

5. What can you catch, but never throw?

6. What goes up and down but never moves?

7. What starts with a 'P', ends with an 'E', and has thousands of letters?

8. I have wings and have a tail, across the sky is where I sail. I have no eyes, ears, or mouth, but I bob from North to South. What am I?

9. If Mr. Blue lives in a blue house, and Mr. Red lives in a red house, who lives in the White House?

10. What has hands but can't clap?

11. What gets wetter and wetter the more it dries?

12. What does Europe and a frying pan have in common?

13. I have keys but no doors. I have space but no rooms. I allow you to enter, but never leave. What am I?

14. The more you take, the more you leave behind. What are they?

15. They come out at night without being called. They are lost in the day without being stolen. What are they?

16. What is so delicate that it's broken when you say its name?

17. What has a neck but no head, and wears a cap?

18. What word has 5 letters but sounds as though it only has 1?

19. What can run but never walks, has a mouth but never talks, has a head but never weeps, has a bed but never sleeps?

20. What goes up but never goes down?

21. What starts with the letter T, is filled with T, and ends in a T?

22. What invention allows people to look through walls?

23. Sarah's mother has three daughters. The first is called Jess, the second is called Rebecca. What is the third daughter's name?

24. What never asks questions but is often answered?

25. What belongs to you, but is used more by others?

26. What has 4 legs but can't walk?

27. What can be big, white, dirty, and wicked?

28. What has a thumb and four fingers, but isn't alive?

29. What weighs more, a pound of feathers, or a pound of bricks?

30. What comes once in a minute, twice in a moment, but not once in a thousand years?

31. What do the numbers 11, 69, and 88 all have in common?

32. I am an odd number. Take away 1 letter and I become even. What am I?

33. If two's company and three's a crown, what are four and five?

34. What word begins and ends with E, but only has 1 letter?

35. Can you name 4 days of the week that start with the letter 'T'?

36. What can run but never walk?

37. What's full of holes but still holds water?

38. What has 1 eye but can't see?

39. What word looks the same both backwards and upside down?

40. What 5 letter word becomes shorter when you add 2 letters to it?

41. The one who made it, didn't want it. The one who bought it, didn't use it. The one who used it, never saw it. What is it?

42. What needs an answer but doesn't ask a question?

43. Forward I am heavy, but backwards I am not. What am I?

44. If I have it, I don't share it. If I share it, I don't have it. What is it?

45. A cowboy rides into town on Friday, stays for 3 days, then leaves on Friday. How did it he do it?

46. How many months have 28 days?

47. I'm tall when I'm young and short when I'm old. What am I?

48. Where can you find cities, towns, streets, and shops, but no people?

49. What has a bottom at the top?

50. What has a face and two hands, but not arms or legs?

51. What's black and white and read all over?

52. If you walk into a dark room that contains a match, a kerosene lamp, a candle, and a fireplace. Which should you light first?

53. Who can shave 20 times a day but still have a beard?

54. Everyone has one, but they can never lose it. What is it?

55. What has one head, one foot, and four legs?

56. What gets bigger the more you take away?

57. What's bright orange with green on top, and sounds like a parrot?

58. What's easy to get into, but hard to get out of?

59. What word contains 26 letters but only 3 syllables?

60. What has lots of eyes but can't see?

61. What can you break without touching it?

62. I have to be opened, but I don't have any key or lid. What am I?

63. What kind of cup doesn't hold any water?

64. I am always in front of you, and never behind. What am I?

65. What kind of band never plays music?

66. I have many teeth but cannot bite. What am I?

67. What has a neck but no head?

68. What type of cheese is made backwards?

69. Which letter of the alphabet has the most water?

70. What has to be broken before it can be used?

71. Where does Friday come before Thursday?

72. What type of ship has 2 mates but no captain?

73. Jimmy throws a ball as hard as he can. Nobody else touches it, yet it comes right back to him. How is that possible?

74. What kind of tree can you carry in your hand?

75. Which word in the dictionary is spelled incorrectly?

76. What can you keep after giving it to someone?

77. A man dies of old age on his 25th birthday. How is that possible?

78. What has branches but no trunk, leaves, or fruit?

79. The more there is, the less you see. What is it?

80. What has many keys but can't open any locks?

81. I'm lighter than a feather, yet not even the strongest man can hold me for 10 minutes. What am I?

82. What goes up and down but doesn't move?

83. What has one eye but can't see?

84. What is cut on a table, but never eaten?

85. What runs around a backyard constantly, but never moves?

86. What has many words but never speaks?

87. What can travel around the world without leaving its corner?

88. What has a head and a tail but no body?

89. What building has the most stories?

90. What tastes better than it smells?

91. What has 13 hearts but no other organs?

92. What kind of coat is best put on wet?

93. What has four wheels and flies?

94. What lives in Winter, dies in Summer, and grows its roots upwards?

95. What has three feet but can't walk?

96. What do dogs have that no other animal does?

97. Give me food and I will live. Give me water and I will die. What am I?

98. What room doesn't have any windows?

99. What has hundreds of needles but can't sew?

100. What do you throw out when you want to use it, and take in when you don't want to use it?

101.　　I am so simple that I can only point, yet I direct men all over the world. What am I?

102.　　What question can never be answered with a 'yes'?

103.　　When it's alive, we sing. When it dies, we clap. What is it?

104.　　I make two people out of one. What am I?

105. I blow but don't have lungs. I move things but don't have arms. What am I?

106. A word I know, six letters it contains, remove one and twelve remain. What is it?

107. What can you put in your pocket that keeps it empty?

108. I am white when I am dirty, and black when I am clean. What am I?

109. Where does success come before work?

110. I have no wings, propellers, hands, or feet, yet I soar to the sky. What am I?

111. All around the house with his partner he dances, yet he always works and never romances. What is he?

112. 100 feet in the air but has its back on the ground. What is it?

113. What goes up when rain comes down?

114. What can be picked but not chosen?

Answers

1. Lunch and dinner.

2. Because they don't know the words.

3. A plate.

4. A tennis ball.

5. A cold.

6. The temperature.

7. The post office.

8. A kite.

9. The President.

10. A clock.

11. A towel.

12. They both have Greece at the bottom.

13. A keyboard.

14. Footprints.

15. The stars.

16. Silence.

17. A bottle.

18. Queue.

19. A river.

20. Your age.

21. A teapot.

22. A window.

23. Sarah.

24. A doorbell.

25. Your name.

26. A table.

27. A lie.

28. A glove.

29. Neither, they both weigh 1 pound.

30. The letter 'M'.

31. They read exactly the same when upside down.

32. Seven (remove an 'e' and you get 'even').

33. Nine.

34. Envelope.

35. Tuesday, Thursday, Today, and Tomorrow.

36. Water.

37. A sponge.

38. A needle.

39. SWIMS.

40. Short.

41. A coffin.

42. A telephone.

43. Ton.

44. A secret.

45. His horses' name is Friday.

46. All of them.

47. A candle.

48. A map.

49. Your legs.

50. A clock.

51. A newspaper.

52. The match.

53. A barber.

54. A shadow.

55. A bed.

56. A hole.

57. A carrot.

58. Trouble.

59. Alphabet.

60. A potato.

61. A promise.

62. An egg.

63. A hiccup.

64. Your future.

65. A rubber band.

66. A comb.

67. A bottle.

68. Edam.

69. C.

70. An egg.

71. The dictionary.

72. A relationship.

73. He threw it straight upwards.

74. A palm.

75. Incorrectly.

76. Your word.

77. He was born on February 29th.

78. A bank.

79. Darkness.

80. A piano.

81. Breath.

82. A staircase.

83. A needle.

84. A deck of cards.

85. A fence.

86. A book.

87. A stamp.

88. A coin.

89. The library.

90. Your tongue.

91. A deck of cards.

92. A coat of paint.

93. A garbage truck.

94. An icicle.

95. A yardstick.

96. Puppies.

97. Fire.

98. A mushroom.

99. A porcupine.

100.   An anchor.

101.   A compass.

102.   Are you asleep?

103.   A birthday candle.

104.   A mirror.

105. The wind.

106. Dozens.

107. A hole.

108. A blackboard.

109. The dictionary.

110.   Smoke.

111.   A broom.

112.   A centipede.

113.   An umbrella.

114.   A nose.

Conclusion

Thanks again for choosing this book!

I hope you had fun testing yourself with these fun and tricky riddles.

If you enjoyed them, don't forget to share them with your family and friends!

www.ingramcontent.com/pod-product-compliance
Lightning Source LLC
LaVergne TN
LVHW021739060526
838200LV00052B/3373